# Faith
# **ESSENTIALS**

## Disciple Making Essentials Series

# Ken Adams

# Faith
# ESSENTIALS

ImpactDisciples.com

# BEFORE YOU BEGIN...

One of the essential ingredients for making disciples is a foundation of faith. Every disciple needs to know the basics of the Christian faith. With a faith foundation in place, a disciple can begin to build the life Christ intended for them to have.

Faith Essentials is designed to help you lay a foundation of beliefs and doctrines that are vital to the Christian life. As you work through each of these lessons, remember that the truths in these lessons will help you grow stronger as a disciple of Jesus Christ.

To make the most of this course I recommend the following. First, work hard on each lesson. Take the time needed to work through each weekly lesson. Being prepared will make the weekly group meeting that much more meaningful. Second, read the daily scripture selection each day. If you use the acrostic A.C.T.S. as explained the booklet, you will be amazed at how the Bible will speak to you personally. Third, memorize the weekly memory verse. Each week you will have a verse that will help you grow by memorizing scripture. Don't skip this important part. Finally, be at the group meetings! The group meetings will help you grow even more as you discuss and share what you are learning from God's Word.

In the next several weeks, you will learn essential truths about the Christian faith. These truths will help you stand strong for years to come. I pray that you will soak it all in and allow the Spirit to reveal God's truth to your heart.

Being and Building Disciples,

Ken Adams

# WEEK ONE: WHAT CHRISTIANS BELIEVE ABOUT THE BIBLE

2 Timothy 3:16-17

**Goal:** To understand the doctrine of God's Word.

---

## A STATEMENT OF BELIEF

*We believe the Bible is God's Word to man written by human authors under the supernatural guidance of the Holy Spirit. It is the supreme source of truth for Christian beliefs and living. Being inspired by God, it is truth without any mixture of error.*

The statement of belief written above is based on biblical truth. It is important to know what you believe by understanding the Scripture yourself and not simply by what you have heard from someone else. Take a closer look at what Scripture teaches about the Bible.

### WEEKLY BIBLE READING

Read the passage and write out an insight on at least one of the following:

**A:** Attitude to change
**C:** Command to obey
**T:** Truth to believe
**S:** Sin to confess

☐ **MONDAY**

2 Timothy 3:10-17

## WHAT DOES THE BIBLE SAY?

The Bible makes some very important claims about itself. You must decide whether you believe these claims or not. If you believe them, it will significantly change how you view the Bible. If you believe these claims, it will change the value of the Bible in your life. Take some time to examine the claims the Bible makes.

**The Bible claims to be God's Word!** Write out what Paul said in Galatians 1:11-12. _____

_____

_____

Paul is giving Jesus all the credit for his message. He is clearly claiming that the Scriptures originated in the mind of God and not in the mind of man.

**The Bible claims to be inspired by the Holy Spirit!**

1

Peter 1:21 explain the way the Bible was given to man?

_____

_____

☐ **TUESDAY**
2 Peter 1:16-21

The Bible makes the claim that we received prophecy when the Holy Spirit moved men to speak. The Bible is not merely man's idea; the Bible is God's Word recorded by the supernatural influence of the Holy Spirit.

**The Bible claims to be the ultimate source of truth!** What does Proverbs 30:5 say?_____

_____

The Bible claims to be true and the authority source that we need in order to know how to live our lives. Since the Bible is the Word of God, it is the only real guide you will ever need. As some say, it is the instruction manual for life.

**The Bible claims to be accurate in what it says!** The Bible does not claim to be accurate in a few things; it claims to be accurate in all things. How does Psalm 119:160 affirm this claim?

☐ **WEDNESDAY**
Psalm 119:1-16

_____

_____

Over time, history, archeology, and science all end up confirming the truth of scripture. The "alleged discrepancies" of the Bible are just that — "alleged!" The more you examine the Bible, the more you realize there are no contradictions or discrepancies.

## HOW CAN YOU KNOW IT IS TRUE?

Some critics will say you can't believe the claims of the Bible because they come from the Bible. In other words, they don't think internal evidence is enough to convince them that the Bible's claims are true. If you know someone like that, consider some external evidence that supports the Bible's claims.

The evidence from fulfilled prophecy! One of the

most convincing pieces of evidence for the Bible's claim to be God's Word is the fact that so many biblical prophecies have been fulfilled. In the Old Testament alone, there are over three hundred prophecies concerning Jesus that have all come to pass. Fulfilled prophecy is very convincing evidence.

**The evidence from authenticity!** When compared to all other types of ancient literature, the Bible has more authentic copies of manuscripts than any other writing. This means the Bible is more reliable than any other commonly accepted work of literature.

☐ **THURSDAY**
Hebrews 4:11-16

**The evidence from unity!** The Bible is the most unified book ever written. The sixty-six books, from forty different authors that were written over 1600 years in different languages and locations, all have the same theme. From cover to cover the Bible is totally unified in it's message.

There are several other types of evidence that support the claims the Bible makes to be the Word of God. Taken collectively, it does not take much faith to believe the claims of scripture when supported by the evidence. It actually takes more faith to "not believe" when the evidence for Scripture is examined.

☐ **FRIDAY**
Psalm 119:161-176

If what the Bible claims is true, you need to be reading the Bible every day! What a mistake it would be to let your Bible collect dust on the shelf when it is God's plan to communicate with you.

## YOUR PERSONAL STATEMENT OF BELIEF

A statement of belief means nothing if it is just words you routinely recite. A personal statement of belief will be demonstrated by your actions! If you truly believe that the Bible is God's Word and the supreme source of guidance for life, then you will make it a priority in your life. As you can clearly see, what you believe about the Bible is essential for being a disciple.

## QUESTIONS FOR GROUP DISCUSSION OR PERSONAL REFLECTION

**PRAYER REQUESTS**

_____

_____

_____

_____

_____

_____

_____

_____

_____

_____

_____

_____

_____

_____

_____

_____

_____

➢ Open your group with prayer and share a highlight from your past week.

➢ Take a minute and let people quote this week's memory verse.

➢ What are some of the popular views about the Bible in our world these days?

➢ How does the fact that the Bible claims to be inspired affect the way you read it?

➢ Why is it important to believe the Bible contains no errors?

➢ If the Bible is a supreme source of truth, how does that change the way you look at it?

➢ Does your current level of Bible intake match up with what you say you believe about it?

➢ Take some time to share prayer needs and pray for each other.

# WEEK TWO: WHAT CHRISTIANS BELIEVE ABOUT GOD

**MEMORY VERSE**

Deuteronomy 6:4

**Goal:** To understand the truth about who God is.

---

## A STATEMENT OF BELIEF

*We believe God is the creator and ruler of the universe. He has eternally existed in three persons — the Father, the Son, and the Holy Spirit. These three are co-equal and are one God.*

The doctrine of God is essential for becoming the disciple Christ wants you to be. Although it will take you a lifetime to even begin to gain an understanding of God, there are some basics that you will want to grasp. This lesson will help you grab hold of these simple but important truths.

**WEEKLY BIBLE READING**

Read the passage and write out an insight on at least one of the following:

**A:** Attitude to change
**C:** Command to obey
**T:** Truth to believe
**S:** Sin to confess

## WHAT DOES THE BIBLE SAY?

The Bible is full of information regarding God. So much so that it would take a lifetime to study it all. However, there are a few truths that are essential to a study of what Christians believe about God. Here are a few.

**The Bible assumes the existence of God!** The Bible does not try to prove that God exists. It assumes that He does. The very first phrase in the Bible says, *"In the beginning God."* The Bible is the revelation of God so, therefore, it does not waste any time trying to prove God's existence. What does Psalm 53:1 teach? _____

_____

_____

**The Bible teaches that God is creator and ruler of the universe!** The Bible makes it very clear that everything that exists comes from the hand of God and is ruled by God.

☐ **MONDAY**

Romans 1:18-25

What does Isaiah 40:28 say about God?

**WEEKLY BIBLE READING**

☐ **TUESDAY**
Psalm 90:1-9

_____

_____

**The Bible teaches that God has always existed!**
What does Psalm 90:2 say?_____

_____

_____

Before the world was created, God existed. He is from everlasting to everlasting. That means God has always existed. God is eternal!

**The Bible teaches there is only one God!** There are not a bunch of different gods; there is only one God. In Deuteronomy 6:4, what does the Bible say?_____

_____

_____

**The Bible teaches that God exists as a trinity!** The trinity is very difficult to understand, but we believe it because the Bible clearly teaches it. God exists as God the Father, God the Son, and God the Holy Spirit. He is all three at the same time. There are not three Gods;

☐ **WEDNESDAY**
Deuteronomy 6:1-9

there is one God that exists in a Trinitarian form. How does 2 Corinthians 13:14 reveal the trinity? _____

_____

_____

## HOW CAN YOU KNOW THERE IS A GOD?

The Bible assumes the existence of God, but that is not the only evidence you can look to for the existence of God. Even without the biblical revelation, the existence of God is quite clear. Here are a few examples of how we know God exists from the application of reason.

**Creation demands a creator!** The world around you is either the result of a divine design or random chance. When you look at a watch, you know that a watchmaker produced it and it is not the result of an explosion in a spring factory. In Psalm 102:25 the Psalmist said, "_Of old you laid the foundation of the earth, and the_

6

*heavens are the work of your hands."* The world we live in is evidence for the existence of a creator.

**Conscience calls for a higher power!** There is a sense of right and wrong inside every human being in every culture. God placed this moral compass within each of us. Paul said in Romans 2:15, *"They show that the work of the law is written on their hearts, while their conscience also bears witness, and their conflicting thoughts accuse or even excuse them."* Murder, stealing, and lying are wrong in every culture because God has placed a sense of morality inside every single person. Our conscience is evidence there is a God.

☐ **THURSDAY**
Hebrews 1:1-14

**Worship is evidence for God!** Where did man get the need to worship? Man's need for worship comes from an emptiness inside him that can only be filled by God. Throughout history man has worshiped the sun, the earth, and hundreds of other objects, all of which demonstrate man's need to connect to the true and living God. Ecclesiastes 3:11 says, *"He has put eternity into man's heart."* Man is longing for something more than the "here and now." Man is longing for the "then and there!"

These are just a few of the reasons we can believe that God does exist. In fact, in light of the evidence, it takes more faith not to believe there is a God than it does to believe in Him. The Bible says in Psalm 14:1, *"The fool says in his heart, 'There is no God.'"*

☐ **FRIDAY**
Psalm 19:1-14

## YOUR PERSONAL STATEMENT OF BELIEF

Acknowledging the existence of God is one thing; believing in Him is another. James 2:19 tells us, *"You believe that God is one; you do well. Even the demons believe — and shudder!"* The demons know that God exists, but they have not placed their faith in Him. A personal statement of faith in God comes from the heart, not just the head.

## PRAYER REQUESTS

_____

_____

_____

_____

_____

_____

_____

_____

_____

_____

_____

_____

_____

_____

_____

_____

_____

_____

## QUESTIONS FOR GROUP DISCUSSION OR PERSONAL REFLECTION

➤ Open your group with prayer and share a highlight from your past week.

➤ Take a minute to let people quote this week's memory verse.

➤ What are some of the popular beliefs about God in our world today?

➤ Describe some things we know to be true about God according to the Scriptures.

➤ Read Deuteronomy 6:4 and explain how this verse impacts your faith and belief in God.

➤ Why do you think some people have such a hard time believing that God does exist?

➤ Explain the difference between head knowledge and heart knowledge when it comes to faith in God.

➤ When did you decide that God exists and place your faith in Him?

➤ Take some time to share prayer needs and pray for one another.

# WEEK THREE: WHAT CHRISTIANS BELIEVE ABOUT JESUS

**Goal:** To understand the truth about Jesus.

## MEMORY VERSE
John 14:6

---

## A STATEMENT OF BELIEF

*We believe that Jesus Christ is the Son of God and is co-equal with the Father. Jesus lived a sinless human life and offered Himself as the perfect sacrifice for the sins of all men by dying on a cross. He arose from the dead after three days to demonstrate His power over sin and death. He ascended to heaven's glory and will return again to earth as King of Kings and Lord of Lords.*

What you believe about Jesus is obviously an essential to being a disciple of Christ. The entire Bible points to Jesus, but there are some passages that deal specifically with who Jesus is and what He came to do. We will look at a few of these passages in order to gain a better understanding of what Christians believe about Jesus.

## WEEKLY BIBLE READING

Read the passage and write out an insight on at least one of the following:

**A:** Attitude to change
**C:** Command to obey
**T:** Truth to believe
**S:** Sin to confess

☐ **MONDAY**
John 1:1-18

## WHAT DOES THE BIBLE SAY?

The Bible is the written revelation of a God who became a living revelation. Jesus is the "living word" and we learn a great deal about the "word became flesh" by studying what the written word has to say about His life and ministry. Open your Bible and see what it has to say about Jesus. Having a quiet time where you regularly spend time with God is a great way to build your personal fellowship with God. If you have never practiced a daily quiet time, or if you have gotten slack in doing so, maybe this lesson will help you re-establish this priority in your life.

**The Bible teaches that Jesus is God in the flesh!** The Bible makes it very clear that Jesus was God made man. As the second person of the trinity, Jesus took on

9

flesh and blood and made His dwelling among man. John 1:1 and 14 says, *"In the beginning was the Word, and the Word was with God, and the Word was God...And the Word became flesh and dwelt among us, and we have seen His glory, glory as of the only Son from the Father, full of grace and truth."* What does 1 John 1:2 say? _____

_____

_____

☐ **TUESDAY**
Matthew
1:18-25

**The Bible teaches that Jesus was a sinless and perfect sacrifice!** In 2 Corinthians 5:21, the Bible says this about Jesus: *"For our sake He made Him to be sin who knew no sin, so that in Him we might become the righteousness of God."* Because Jesus was God in the flesh, He could live without sin, and being sinless allowed Him to become to perfect sacrifice for man's sin. What does Hebrews 10:12 say? _____

_____

_____

**The Bible teaches that Jesus rose from the dead and overcame death!** Jesus is not a dead savior; through the resurrection Jesus has become the living Lord. What does Matthew 28:6 say? _____

☐ **WEDNESDAY**
John 14:1-14

_____

_____

How does Romans 6:4 indicate Christ's victory over death? _____

_____

_____

The Bible clearly teaches that Jesus died and rose again. He is alive!

**The Bible teaches that Jesus is in heaven waiting to return to earth!** What happened to Jesus according to Acts 1:9? _____

_____

_____

10

What do the angels claim will happen to Jesus in Acts 1:11? _____

_____

_____

Forty days after the resurrection, Jesus ascended back to heaven, and He waits there interceding on behalf of His children until the day He returns to take them home.

❒ **THURSDAY**
John 20:1-23

## HOW DOES WHAT YOU BELIEVE ABOUT JESUS MATTER?

What you believe about Jesus Christ is a game changer. It is essential! Let's look at how what you believe about Jesus makes an incredible difference in your life.

**More than a man!** If Jesus is not God, you are placing your faith in a simple man. The fact that He is God means you are placing your faith in more than a man. You are trusting in a God that can save you!

**The tomb is empty!** The most important question in life is this: what do you do with the empty tomb? If Jesus' body were still in the tomb, it wouldn't matter what you believe about Jesus, but the fact that the tomb is empty means that Jesus has the power to conquer death.

**Eyewitness accounts!** The Bible tells us that there were numerous post-resurrection appearances of Jesus. These eyewitness accounts were either true or false. Had they been false, Christianity would have died out a long time ago. Billions of lives have been changed because those accounts are true.

❒ **FRIDAY**
Philippians
2:1-11

## YOUR PERSONAL STATEMENT OF BELIEF

You basically have three choices when it comes to what you believe about Jesus. You can say that Jesus was a liar. You can believe that His claim to be God was just a hoax and He fabricated everything He said and did. You can say that Jesus was a lunatic, that He was just a crazy man and nothing He did or said was true. Or, finally, you can believe everything Jesus said and did was true and, as a result, make Him the Lord of your life. That is a personal statement of faith!

# QUESTIONS FOR GROUP DISCUSSION OR PERSONAL REFLECTION

➤ Open your group with prayer and share a victory or struggle you've had this past week.

➤ Take a minute and let everyone quote this week's memory verse.

➤ What are some of the different beliefs concerning Jesus in our world these days?

➤ How does what the Bible teaches about Jesus differ from some of the popular views of Jesus?

➤ How does the fact that Jesus claims to be God affect what you believe about Him?

➤ Why do people have such a hard time believing Jesus rose from the dead, and why do you believe it?

➤ Why does the resurrection mean so much to a Christian?

➤ How does Jesus' promised return impact the way you live your life?

➤ Take some time to share prayer needs and pray for each other.

# WEEK FOUR: WHAT CHRISTIANS BELIEVE ABOUT THE HOLY SPIRIT

**Goal:** To understand the truth about the Holy Spirit.

## A STATEMENT OF BELIEF

*The Holy Spirit is equal with the Father and the Son of God. He is present in the world to make men aware of their need for Jesus Christ. He also lives in every Christian from the moment of salvation. He provides the Christian with power for living, understanding of spiritual truth, and guidance in doing what is right. The Christian should seek to live under His control on a daily basis.*

There are so many different teachings regarding the Holy Spirit within the church these days that it can be hard for anyone to truly know what a Christian believes about the Spirit. The important thing is to look at what is clearly taught concerning the Holy Spirit within the Scriptures. This lesson will help clear some of the confusion in regards to the Holy Spirit.

### WEEKLY BIBLE READING

Read the passage and write out an insight on at least one of the following:

**A:** Attitude to change
**C:** Command to obey
**T:** Truth to believe
**S:** Sin to confess

☐ **MONDAY**
John 14:15-31

## WHAT DOES THE BIBLE SAY?

The Bible makes many clear references to the person and the work of the Holy Spirit. As you look at a few of these references, remember to separate what the Bible clearly says from some of the confusion created by man.

**The Holy Spirit is God!** One of the first truths concerning the Holy Spirit is that the Holy Spirit is God in the form of a Spirit. This means the Holy Spirit is not an "it" or a "thing." The Holy Spirit is a "He." The Holy Spirit is God.

In Acts 5:3 who did Ananias lie to?_____
Peter clearly tells Ananias that he lied to God. What does Peter say about Ananias in Acts 5:4? _____

_____

Peter used the names Holy Spirit and God synonymously because they are one and the same! Clearly the Holy Spirit is God.

**The Holy Spirit convicts nonbelievers!** One of the roles of the Holy Spirit is to make people realize their need for Christ. The Holy Spirit convicts a person of their sin and their need for forgiveness. What does Jesus teach concerning the Holy Spirit in John 16:8? _____

_____

Clearly the Holy Spirit is the one who reveals a person's sin and their need for Christ. What happened to a woman named Lydia in Acts 16:14? _____

_____

How did the Lord open her heart to pay attention to Paul's words? _____

_____

**The Holy Spirit resides in every believer!** The moment a person receives Christ into their life as Lord and Savior, the Holy Spirit takes up residence inside their spirit. What do we receive the moment we believe in Christ according to Acts 2:38? _____

_____

In 1 Corinthians 12:13 Paul says that *"all [believers]"* are baptized into one body. The idea that some believers have the Spirit and some don't is clearly not the teaching of scripture.

**The Holy Spirit controls a yielded believer!** It is possible for a Christian to be indwelt by the Holy Spirit and not be controlled by the Holy Spirit. Obviously, this is not what God intends, but the Holy Spirit will not override a person's will and desire to submit to His control. In Ephesians 5:18 the Bible clearly teaches that every believer is to be *"filled"* with the Spirit. To be filled by the Holy Spirit is to let the Spirit have control of your life on a daily basis.

☐ **TUESDAY**
Acts 1:1-11

☐ **WEDNESDAY**
1 Corinthians
2:1-16

14

## HOW DOES THE HOLY SPIRIT IMPACT YOUR LIFE?

When you are living under the control of the Holy Spirit , He will work in and through your life in some amazing ways. Here are just a few examples of how the Holy Spirit impacts the life of a believer.

❑ **THURSDAY**
Galatians
5:16-26

**The Holy Spirit produces fruit!** One by-product of the Spirit controlling a believer is that He produces spiritual fruit in the life of a Christian. How is this described in Galatians 5:22-23? _____

_____

The fruit of the Spirit is the character of Christ on display in the life of a believer.

**The Holy Spirit provides gifts!** The Holy Spirit distributes spiritual gifts to believers. What are the gifts Paul mentions in Romans 12:6-8?_____

_____

God gives these spiritual gifts to be used in building His kingdom. If you are a believer, you have a gift that needs to be used. What did Peter say in 1 Peter 4:10? ____

_____

❑ **FRIDAY**
Ephesians
1:3-14

**The Holy Spirit gives guidance!** The Holy Spirit speaks to the believer and uses the Word of God and the people of God to make you more like the Son of God. When you ask God to lead you, He does so through the leadings of His Spirit. Look at what happened to Paul in Acts 16:6-7. The Holy Spirit led Paul in a different direction.

## YOUR PERSONAL STATEMENT OF BELIEF

What a person believes about the Holy Spirit is usually demonstrated in their lifestyle. A person that believes the Holy Spirit is God and controls the believer is typically behaving in a way that reflects that belief, or at least feeling convicted that they are not. The person that does not believe what the Bible teaches about the Holy Spirit is usually not honoring God and doesn't care. In both cases, it is a personal statement of faith.

**PRAYER
REQUESTS**

➤ Open your group with prayer and share a highlight from your week.

➤ Take a few minutes and let everyone quote the memory verse.

➤ What do you think most nonbelievers think about the Holy Spirit?

➤ What are some of the different views believers have regarding the Spirit?

➤ Why is it important to understand that the Holy Spirit is God?

➤ How did the Holy Spirit convict you of your need for Christ?

➤ What does it mean to be living under the influence of the Holy Spirit?

➤ Have you ever experienced a leading of the Holy Spirit in your life? Explain.

➤ How can the fruit of the Spirit, displayed in believer's lives, change the world we live in?

➤ Take some time to share prayer needs and pray for each other.

# WEEK FIVE: WHAT CHRISTIANS BELIEVE ABOUT MAN

**Goal:** To understand the truth about mankind.

## MEMORY VERSE

Romans 3:23

## A STATEMENT OF BELIEF

*Man is made in the spiritual image of God to be like Him in character. He is the supreme object of God's creation. Although man has tremendous potential for good, he is marred by an attitude of disobedience toward God called "sin." This attitude separates man from God.*

Mankind is a mess! Like sheep, man is prone to wander and prone to leave the God that created him. Jesus looked at the multitudes and said they were harassed and helpless, like sheep without a shepherd. Understanding how man lost his way is essential to being a disciple of Jesus Christ. Let's take a look at what the Bible says about man.

## WEEKLY BIBLE READING

Read the passage and write out an insight on at least one of the following:

**A:** Attitude to change
**C:** Command to obey
**T:** Truth to believe
**S:** Sin to confess

☐ **MONDAY**

Genesis 1:26-31

The Bible is a story about God and man. It tells us how man got here, why he is here, how he lost his way, and how he can find it again. Man's story cannot be separated from God's story. God's story is about His relationship with man. Let's take some time to examine some of the main truths regarding what the Bible says about man.

**Man was created in the image of God!** What does Genesis 1:27 say about man? _____

_____

Since the Bible tells us that God is a Spirit (John 4:24), to be made in God's image is not referring to a physical image but rather a moral, mental, and relational image. Being created in God's image refers to the immaterial part of man. Being created in God's image sets man apart from the animals over which God gave him dominion. Man is created with a likeness that allows him to relate and fellowship with his Creator.

**Man was created to have a love relationship with God!** What does Genesis 3:8 teach you about man?_____

**WEEKLY BIBLE READING**

_____

☐ **TUESDAY**
Genesis 3:1-13

Man was made to be in relationship with God. God is a relational God and a God of love, and man was created to be the recipient of God's love. In Colossians 1:16 the Bible says, *"All things were created through Him and for Him."* God did not create man because He needed man, but rather because He wanted to have a relationship with man. Like a child is created as an object of two parent's love, we have been created to be the object of the Father's love.

**Man's relationship with God is marred by sin!** What does Isaiah 43:7 say? _____

_____

What does Romans 3:23 say? _____

_____

☐ **WEDNESDAY**
Isaiah 53:1-6

Man was created for God's glory, but sin has caused man to fall short of God's glory. Sin makes it impossible for man to fulfill his purpose and bring glory to God. Sin has broken man's relationship with God and separated him from God.

**Man's sin separates him from God!** What does Romans 5:12 say? _____

_____

Sin not only separates man from God during his life, it also separates Him from God for all eternity. Romans 6:23 said, *"For the wages of sin is death."* Since man is separated from God by sin, he has lost his purpose in life. Instead of living to bring God glory, apart from God, man seeks to glorify himself.

## HOW DOES MAN'S CONDITION IMPACT US?

The fact that man has sinned and broken his relationship with God has ramifications for all of us. Living in a separated relationship from our Creator causes man to be and do things he was never intended to do. We need to understand how man's sin has impacted everyone.

**God wanted man to want to love Him!** God did not make man to be robots and love Him because they were made to do so. God created man with free will and gave him the opportunity to choose to obey Him and follow Him. In Genesis 2:16-17 what choice did God give Adam and Eve? _____

❒ **THURSDAY**
Romans 3:21-31

_____

**Man is born with a God-shaped hole inside!** As a result of Adam's disobedience, every person is born with a spiritual hole in his or her soul that only God can fill. This hole is very obvious because man is constantly trying to fill it with everything but God. How is this hole described in Genesis 3:10? _____

_____

Man's guilt is an indication of the emptiness he has inside. Only a right relationship with God through Christ can fill that spiritual hole.

**God loves man, but He hates sin!** Because God is a holy God, He cannot tolerate and accept sin. It is God's holiness that causes a separation between Creator and creation. What does 1 Peter 1:16 say about God? _____

❒ **FRIDAY**
Psalm 51:1-19

_____

## YOUR PERSONAL STATEMENT OF BELIEF

Every time you start feeling guilty because you have done something wrong, you affirm your belief about man. If that guilt was not present we might need to go back and rewrite the statement of faith that began this lesson. The fact that guilt is very real is evidence of the fact that man has sinned and fallen short of the glory of God.

## QUESTIONS FOR GROUP DISCUSSION
## OR PERSONAL REFLECTION

☛ Open your group with prayer and share one thing God has been teaching you recently.

☛ Take some time to let everyone quote this week's memory verse.

☛ What do you think the popular views of man are today?

☛ Describe God's original plan for a relationship with man.

☛ How and why has sin changed man's relationship with God?

☛ Did you ever feel like you had a God-shaped hole inside? Explain.

☛ What does the presence of "guilt" tell us about our relationship with God?

☛ How do you think God feels about man's spiritual condition?

☛ Take some time to share prayer needs and pray for each other.

# WEEK SIX: WHAT CHRISTIANS BELIEVE ABOUT SALVATION

**Goal:** To understand the truth about salvation.

## A STATEMENT OF BELIEF

*Salvation is a gift from God to man. Man can never make up for his sin by self-improvement or good works. Only by trusting in Jesus Christ as God's offer for forgiveness can man be saved from sin's penalty. Eternal life begins the moment one receives Jesus Christ into his life by faith.*

Everyone wants to know that they have salvation and will spend the rest of eternity in heaven with God, but not everyone agrees on how that happens. There is so much riding on the doctrine of salvation that it is essential for you to know the truth about this belief. The important thing is what the Bible teaches about salvation, and not what others might say about salvation.

**WEEKLY BIBLE READING**

Read the passage and write out an insight on at least one of the following:

**A:** Attitude to change
**C:** Command to obey
**T:** Truth to believe
**S:** Sin to confess

◻ **MONDAY**
Romans 5:1-11

The Bible gives very clear instruction about how a person can be sure of their salvation. God does not want your salvation to be a guessing game. He wants you to be saved and certain that you are! Let's examine what the Bible says about the subject of salvation.

**Salvation is a free gift from God!** What does Romans 6:23 say about salvation?_____

_____

The fact that salvation is a free gift means that there are no strings attached. When someone gives you a gift, the only action required on your part is to receive it. You don't pay for a gift or work for a gift. You simply accept it. Christ makes salvation a gift to every person. Receiving it is up to you. If you receive it, you will have eternal life. If you reject it, you choose eternal death.

**Salvation is not a result of self-effort!** No one can save himself or herself. No matter how good you are or how much you do for God, it will never be enough to gain salvation. What does Paul say in Ephesians 2:8-9?___

___

A person is saved purely on the basis of grace. Grace is God's unmerited favor. A person is saved not because they deserved it but because God gives them better than they deserve.

**Salvation comes through faith in Christ!** Salvation is by faith in Christ alone. What does Romans 5:1 say?___

___

There is only one way to have salvation. Only through faith in Jesus Christ can a person be saved for all of eternity. Jesus said that He is the way, the truth, and the life, and no one comes to the Father except through Him. This is a claim that Jesus made Himself. This claim excludes all other means of salvation. Only Jesus paid the debt that is sufficient for salvation.

**Salvation begins one's eternal life!** Eternal life begins the moment a person trusts in Jesus not just when a person dies. John 17:3 says, *"And this is eternal life, that they know you the only true God, and Jesus Christ whom you have sent."* In other words, the moment you receive Christ's offer for salvation, you begin to live for all eternity. Your body will die someday but your soul will live forever. When did your eternal life begin? _____

___

___

## HOW DOES THE TRUTH ABOUT SALVATION AFFECT YOU?

The clear instruction from the Scripture about salvation causes us to draw several important conclusions. These conclusions help us to understand why certain people miss the truth about salvation, and help us be certain we don't miss it ourselves.

**God never sends people to hell!** The person that rejects Christ's offer of salvation chooses to spend an eternity separated from God rather than an eternity in the presence of God. Never once has God sent a person into eternal punishment. A person sends himself or herself into eternal punishment by choosing to reject Christ's free gift. How is hell described in Mark 9:48?____

❑ **THURSDAY**
1 John 1:1-10

_____

_____

**All religions can't be right!** Jesus made a claim to be the only way to God. This means He is either right or wrong. The interesting thing is that every other religion makes a claim of how to get to God as well. Since all of these claims are different from what Christ claimed, they can all be wrong but they cannot all be right. What does John 14:6 say?_____

_____

**Faith is active not passive!** I once heard about a tightrope walker who pushed a wheelbarrow across a tightrope. Once he completed the walk, he asked his crowd if they thought he could do the same thing with a person sitting in the wheelbarrow? Every hand in the crowd went up, and then he asked who would be willing to get in it. No one moved! What does James 2:18 teach?

❑ **FRIDAY**
1 John 4:7-21

_____

## YOUR PERSONAL STATEMENT OF BELIEF

Placing your faith in Christ does not have to be "blind faith." There is a tremendous amount of evidence that supports the claims of Jesus Christ. You can place faith in Christ with a great amount of reason behind your faith. In fact, the evidence for placing your faith in Christ is so strong that you would actually need more faith to reject Christ's claims than to accept them. Only a fool would reject the evidence supporting the claims of Christ.

## QUESTIONS FOR GROUP DISCUSSION OR PERSONAL REFLECTION

**PRAYER REQUESTS**

_____

_____

_____

_____

_____

_____

_____

_____

_____

_____

_____

_____

_____

_____

_____

_____

_____

_____

_____

_____

➤ Open your group with prayer and share a victory or a struggle that you have had in the past week.

➤ Take some time to let everyone quote this week's memory verse.

➤ Why do so many people think there is more than one way to God?

➤ Why is grace such a difficult concept to grasp?

➤ Describe the difference between believing with your head and believing with your heart.

➤ Explain how salvation begins one's eternal life.

➤ How did salvation happen for you personally?

➤ Why is it impossible to "work your way" into heaven?

➤ How would you respond to someone who says, "It doesn't matter what you believe as long as you believe?"

➤ Take some time to share prayer needs and pray for each other.

# WEEK SEVEN: WHAT CHRISTIANS BELIEVE ABOUT ETERNITY

**Goal:** To understand the truth about eternity.

**MEMORY VERSE**

1 John 2:25

---

## A STATEMENT OF BELIEF

*Man was created to exist forever. He will either exist eternally separated from God by sin or in union with God through forgiveness and salvation. To be eternally separated from God is hell. To be eternally in union with Him is eternal life. Heaven and hell are both literal places of eternal existence.*

People are either fascinated by the idea of eternity or they reject it totally. However, one thing is for sure, no one is neutral when it comes to eternity. We all want to know what eternity will be like and where we will spend it. If you accept the belief that everyone exists for eternity, then knowing the truth about it should be a major priority. You need to learn all you can about eternity because you are going to be there a very long time!

**WEEKLY BIBLE READING**

Read the passage and write out an insight on at least one of the following:

**A:** Attitude to change
**C:** Command to obey
**T:** Truth to believe
**S:** Sin to confess

☐ **MONDAY**
John 14:1-7

## WHAT DOES THE BIBLE SAY?

The Bible is not silent in regards to eternity. The Bible is clear that man lives for eternity in one of two possible locations. The only problem when it comes to learning about eternity is separating fact from fiction. There is so much misinformation regarding eternity that it is essential that you discover what the Bible teaches about it.

**Everyone exists forever!** Everyone will die a physical death. After bodily death occurs, everyone will exist for eternity in either a place called heaven or a place called hell. What does Ecclesiastes 3:11 say?_____

_____

God has put eternity in man's heart! Everyone longs to live for eternity because God has created us to exist forever. The question is where will you exist for eternity?

What two eternal locations are mentioned in Matthew 25:46? _____

_____

**Heaven is a place of eternal life with God!** The Bible teaches that heaven is a literal place of eternal life where people who accept Christ will spend the rest of eternity enjoying the presence of God. What does 1 John 5:12-13 say? _____

_____

_____

How is heaven described in Revelation 21:3-4? _____

_____

Heaven will be the perfect place to dwell with God for the rest of eternity!

**Hell is a place of eternal death without God!** The Bible indicates that hell is a literal place of eternal death where people who reject Christ will spend all of eternity separated from the presence of God. How is hell described in Matthew 25:41? _____

_____

_____

What will happen in the future according to Revelation 20:10?

_____

Hell will be the worst place a person can be for the rest of eternity!

**A person's eternal destiny is determined before he or she physically dies!** Where a person will spend their eternity is determined by the choice they make while they are still physically alive. Jesus made this decision crystal clear in John 11:25-26. What did Jesus say? _____

_____

## HOW DOES THE TRUTH ABOUT ETERNITY IMPACT YOUR LIFE?

The truth about the "then and there" has an incredible impact on how you live "here and now." When you consider the fact that everyone will exist for all of eternity in a place called heaven or in a place called hell, you cannot be neutral about eternity. Let's consider some of the ramifications with regards to eternity.

**Earth is only temporary!** The fact that the Bible teaches man's eternal existence is a good reminder that this life is only temporary. What does 2 Corinthians 4:18 say? _____

_____

❑ **THURSDAY**
2 Corinthians
5:1-10

The problems you face in this life are nothing compared to eternity.

**Eternity is a long time to be wrong!** If what the Bible teaches about eternity is not true, then it doesn't really matter how you live "here and now." On the other hand, if what the Bible says about eternity is true, then that changes everything! It changes how you live this life, and it changes what you share with others. Knowing that people will live in heaven or hell should cause you to want to be certain about your own eternal destination, and it should also make you care about the eternal destination of others. How is this expressed in Acts 16:31?___

_____

❑ **FRIDAY**
Revelation
21:1-8

Eternity should make us concerned about where we are headed and who is going there with us.

## YOUR PERSONAL STATEMENT OF BELIEF

There is one word that truly indicates what a person believes about eternity. It is the word "hope!" If we have heaven to look forward to, then we have hope. With heaven in your future, this life is as bad as it is ever going to be. What did Paul say in 1 Thessalonians 4:13-14? ____

_____

The resurrection of Jesus and the truth of heaven give a believer so much to look forward to. We may mourn when people die, but we do not lose hope!

## QUESTIONS FOR GROUP DISCUSSION OR PERSONAL REFLECTION

➤ Open your group with prayer and share something the Lord has done in your life this past week.

➤ Take some time to let everyone quote this week's memory verse.

➤ What are some different views of eternity that exist in the world today?

➤ What are some things the Bible tells us about heaven? About hell?

➤ How can a person be sure about his or her eternal destination?

➤ How does the Bible's teaching on eternity changes how you face life's trials?

➤ How does the biblical view of eternity give us hope in the face of death?

➤ Who is someone you'd really like to see in heaven some day?

➤ Take some time to share prayer needs and pray for each other.

# A FEW FINAL THOUGHTS...

Now that you have finished *Faith Essentials,* you should have a good foundation on what you believe. Now that you know some of the essentials of Christian beliefs, keep seeking Him and living out your personal statement of beliefs daily!

To keep growing as a disciple, consider working through another course in the Disciple Making Essentials Series. You may also want to check out more resources from Impact Ministries. Check out the Impact Ministries page in the back of this booklet or look us up on the web at impactdisciples.com. To sign up for our monthly e-news, go to our website and sign up there, impactdisciples.com.

# KEEP THE FAITH!

 Inspiring People and Churches to Be and Build Disciples of Jesus Christ

# EXPLORE

We invite you to EXPLORE and DISCOVER the concepts of DISCIPLE MAKING by checking out the following RESOURCES.
◆The Impact Blog ◆The Impact Newsletter
◆The Impact Audio and Video Podcasts

# EDUCATE

We encourage you to LEARN more about DISCIPLE MAKING through our written RESOURCES and TRAINING opportunities.
◆The DMC Training ◆315 Leadership Training ◆Free Resources

# ESTABLISH

We seek to HELP you start a DISCIPLE MAKING MOVEMENT by showing you how to LAUNCH a disciple making group.
◆The Impact Weekend ◆The Essentials ◆Vision Consultation

# ENGAGE

We invite you to JOIN with Impact Ministries in spreading the VISION of DISCIPLE MAKING around the WORLD through several involvement opportunities.
◆Join our Prayer Team ◆Be an Impact Trainer ◆Partner with Us

# CONTACT US

◆ImpactDisciples.com ◆Info@ImpactDisciples.com ◆678.854.9322

Made in the USA
Columbia, SC
16 September 2019